Channel Islands National Marine Sanctuary, *Okeanos Explorer* Cruise, 2011 Taxonomic Guide

Danielle Lipski[1] and Jennifer L. Bright[2]

[1]Channel Islands National Marine Sanctuary
113 Harbor Way, Suite 150
Santa Barbara, CA 93109

[2]Olympic Coast National Marine Sanctuary
115 East Railroad Avenue, Suite 301
Port Angeles, WA 98362-2925

U.S. Department of Commerce
Penny Pritzker, Secretary

National Oceanic and Atmospheric Administration
Kathryn Sullivan, Ph.D.
Acting Under Secretary of Commerce for Oceans and Atmosphere

National Ocean Service
Holly Bamford, Ph.D., Assistant Administrator

Silver Spring, Maryland
August 2013

Office of National Marine Sanctuaries
Daniel J. Basta, Director

Disclaimer

Report content does not necessarily reflect the views and policies of the Office of National Marine Sanctuaries or the National Oceanic and Atmospheric Administration, nor does the mention of trade names or commercial products constitute endorsement or recommendation for use.

Report Availability

Electronic copies of this report may be downloaded from the Office of National Marine Sanctuaries web site at http://sanctuaries.noaa.gov. Hard copies may be available from the following address:

National Oceanic and Atmospheric Administration
Office of National Marine Sanctuaries
SSMC4, N/ORM62
1305 East-West Highway
Silver Spring, MD 20910

Cover

Clockwise from top left: *Heterochone calyx* goiter sponge, *Anthomastus* sp., *Apristurus brunneus*, ruffled white sponge (NOAA/CINMS 2011)

Suggested Citation

Lipski, D., J.L. Bright. 2013. Taxonomic Guide. Marine Sanctuaries Conservation Series ONMS-13-06. U.S. Department of Commerce, National Oceanic and Atmospheric Administration, Office of National Marine Sanctuaries, Silver Spring, MD. 60 pp.

Contact

Danielle Lipski, Channel Islands National Marine Sanctuary, 113 Harbor Way, Suite 150, Santa Barbara, CA 93109, 805-966-7107, Danielle.Lipski@noaa.gov or Jennifer Bright, Olympic Coast National Marine Sanctuary, 115 East Railroad Avenue, Suite 301, Port Angeles, Washington, 98362-2925, 360-457-6622, Jennifer.Bright@noaa.gov

TABLE OF CONTENTS

ABSTRACT

This is the first taxonomic guide of deep sea organisms for the Channel Islands National Marine Sanctuary. From April 21 to 27, 2011, the NOAA ship *Okeanos Explorer* started their field season with a shakedown cruise primarily to field test equipment. The cruise also provided an opportunity to conduct multibeam mapping and a series of exploratory dives using the Little Hercules Remotely Operated Vehicle (ROV) in Channel Islands National Marine Sanctuary. The ROV explored areas that had not been surveyed previously. Video of these opportunistic dives was analyzed for habitat types, species, and species associations. The species observations from the dives are recorded in this taxonomic guide to provide baseline characterization for this underexplored habitat in the sanctuary. This guide will be amended as more studies are added or completed.

KEY WORDS

Channel Islands National Marine Sanctuary, *Okeanos Explorer*, deep sea, corals, sponges, fishes, invertebrates, taxonomy.

INTRODUCTION

In April 2011, the NOAA Ship *Okeanos Explorer* began its field season with a shakedown cruise through Channel Islands National Marine Sanctuary (CINMS). The mission of this cruise (number EX1101) was focused on preparing for the upcoming field season by testing equipment such as sonar, a remotely operated vehicle (ROV), and other supporting equipment.

In the process of meeting the shakedown objectives, there were opportunities to conduct multibeam sonar mapping and ROV dives in southern California, including areas within the Channel Islands National Marine Sanctuary. Onboard seafloor mapping personnel collaborated with scientists from the Office of National Marine Sanctuaries (ONMS) to map and conduct ROV dives in or near the sanctuary (Figure 1).

After the cruise, videos recorded by the ROV were analyzed for habitat types, fishes and invertebrates and species associations. Seventy-nine benthic and mid-water taxa were observed from the video and are presented in this taxonomic guide, providing the first inventory of deep water communities in CINMS.

METHODS

The exploration cruise EX1101 provided an opportunity to test systems and equipment prior to integrating the use of the Little Hercules remotely operated vehicle (ROV). The cruise also provided an opportunity to conduct bathymetric mapping and to select dive targets for ROV testing for subsequent cruises.

The *Okeanos Explorer* is the only ship in the NOAA fleet to have a dedicated ROV. The ship is also equipped with an integrated control room for operating the multibeam sonar, ROV and telepresence communication equipment. The Little Hercules is a 4000m depth rated ROV and came to the *Okeanos Explorer* through collaboration between NOAA's Office of Ocean Exploration and Research and Dr. Robert Ballard's Institute for Exploration at the University of Rhode Island (IFE). The ROV dives were exploratory rather than predetermined transects, sizing lasers were not used, specimens were not collected, and video was collected discontinuously. The video system on the Little Hercules ROV has two single chip color CCD cameras, two LED lights, two 400 watt HMI lights and a state-of-the-art high definition video camera, all of which provides high quality imagery.

This taxonomic guide follows a similar format to the Davidson Seamount Taxonomic Guide (Burton, E., L. Lundsten. 2008). Video clips from the seven ROV dives conducted in or near CINMS were annotated using Monterey Bay Aquarium Research Institute's (MBARI) Video Annotation and Reference System (VARS) (Lipski et al 2013). All images in this guide are frame grabs extracted from the video and species are identified to the lowest possible taxon. Images of taxa were provisionally identified by J. Bright and sent to additional experts for further confirmation. Some of the images are pending taxa identification from the experts and will remain provisional until confirmed. Also, some species were not known and will remain provisional or the species could not be confirmed from the video. This taxonomic guide will remain a work in progress as species are added and identified.

ABOUT THE SANCTUARY

In 1980, a portion of the Santa Barbara Channel was given a special protected status with the designation of the Channel Islands National Marine Sanctuary (Figure 1). The sanctuary is an area of national significance because of its exceptional natural beauty and resources. It encompasses approximately 1,470 square miles (or 1,110 square nautical miles) of water surrounding Anacapa, Santa Cruz, Santa Rosa, San Miguel and Santa Barbara Islands, extending from mean high tide to six nautical miles offshore around each of the five islands. The sanctuary's primary goal is the protection of the natural and cultural resources contained within its boundaries.

USING THIS GUIDE

Taxonomic pages in this guide begin with the appropriate classification scheme followed by an image and identification information side by side (Table 1). The taxonomic classification is continued from the header, listing the scientific name down to the lowest taxonomic identification determined. It also lists the common name, the person making the preliminary identification, the person making the identification confirmation, and whether the image identification can be confirmed from video. The dive reports for this survey only list an approximate depth for each dive location so images reflect the depth of the particular dive where the frame grab was taken.

As previously stated, organisms were identified to the lowest taxonomic level. If an organism could not be identified beyond the genus level, the lowest genus was presented in capital letters, with the epithet "sp." Or "species," and numbered if more than one observation was made and differentiated (e.g., PORIFERA species 1, PORIFERA species 2). If more than one taxon was likely present by could not be differentiated, the epthet "spp." was used (e.g., ZOARCIDAE spp.). In this case, a representative image was provided.

Well established common names are provided where appropriate. Some descriptive common names were also provided where a common name could not be used. These descriptive names were given until a further identification is determined.

The references used to classify organisms in this guide are cited in the *References*.

The people who assisted with identification of organisms are cited (in alphabetical order) in the *Personal Communications* portion of the guide.

Ability to identify organisms from Video
Descriptions of how identifiable video images were determined are as follows:

Confirmed: This organism has been identified from video (as certain as they can be without a specimen) by a taxonomic expert.

Provisional: This organism is likely to be this taxon based on an investigation by video analyst (literature search, consultation with outside taxonomic experts, etc.).

Unconfirmed: The identification of this organism cannot be confidently determined from video.

Table 1. An example of the guide format and a brief explanation of the notation.

Phylum *Class* *Order*	
Image	*Further classification (e.g., Family)* *Scientific name* *Common name* *Preliminary Classification* *Identification Confirmation* *Video Identifiability* *Approximate depth range in meters (m)*
Image Credit	

Figure 1. Location of ROV dives in the Channel Islands National Marine Sanctuary.
Credit: CINMS

TAXONOMIC GUIDE

1. Phylum: PORIFERA – sponge morphs

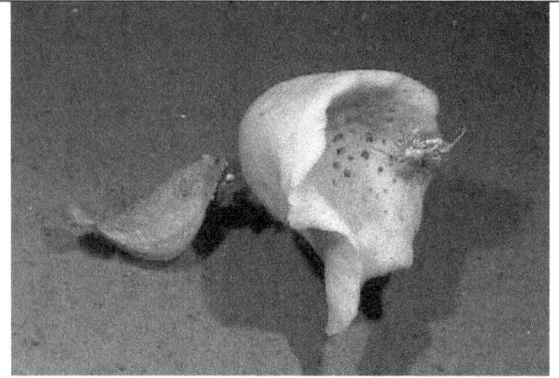

Credit: NOAA/CINMS 2011

PORIFERA species 1
Sponge, stalked morph (pink)

Preliminary Classification: J. Bright
Identification Confirmation:
Video Identifiability: Provisional

Approximate Depth: 886m

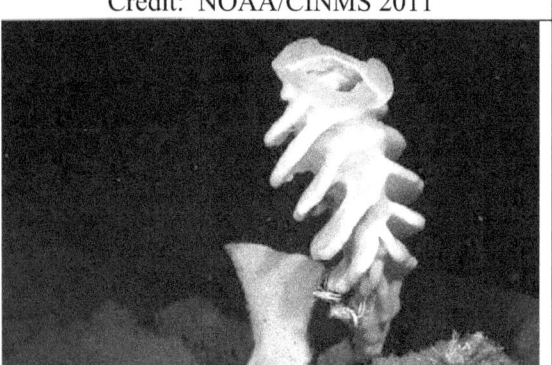

Credit: NOAA/CINMS 2011

PORIFERA species 2
sponge, scalloped morph (white)

Preliminary Classification: J. Bright
Identification Confirmation:
Video Identifiability: Provisional

Approximate Depth: 786m

Credit: NOAA/CINMS 2011

PORIFERA species 3
sponge cylindrical morph (white)

Preliminary Classification: J. Bright
Identification Confirmation:
Video Identifiability: Provisional

Approximate Depth: 786m

1. Phylum: PORIFERA – sponge morphs (cont'd)

 Credit: NOAA/CINMS 2011	PORIFERA species 4 sponge, cylindrical morph (hairy or boot) (possibly *Rhabdocalyptus dawsoni*) Preliminary Identification: J. Bright Identification Confirmation: Video Identifiability: Provisional Approximate Depth: 886m
 Credit: NOAA/CINMS 2011	PORIFERA species 5 sponge, globular morph (yellow) Preliminary Identification: J. Bright Identification Confirmation: Video Identifiability: Provisional Approximate Depth: 803m
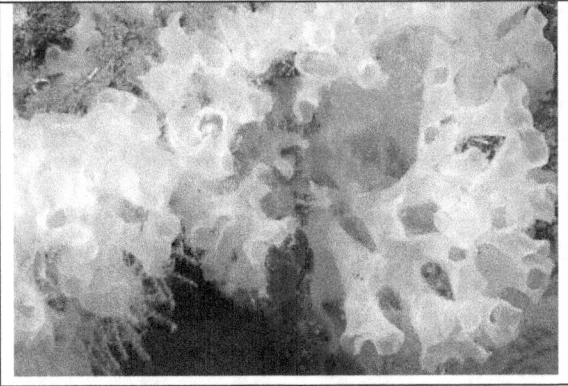 Credit: NOAA/CINMS 2011	PORIFERA species 6 sponge, ruffled morph (white) (possibly - *Farrea* sp.) Preliminary Identification: J. Bright Identification Confirmation: Video Identifiability: Provisional Approximate Depth: 745m

1. Phylum: PORIFERA – sponge morphs (cont'd)

Credit: NOAA/CINMS 2011

PORIFERA species 7
sponge, vase (white)

Preliminary Identification: J. Bright
Identification Confirmation:
Video Identifiability: Provisional

Approximate Depth: 786m

Credit: NOAA/CINMS 2011

PORIFERA species 8
sponge, columnar (yellow)

Preliminary Identification: J. Bright
Identification Confirmation:
Video Identifiability: Provisional

Approximate Depth: 745m

1. Phylum: PORIFERA – sponges
1.1. Class: Demospongiae
1.1.1. Order: Poecilosclerida
1.1.1.1. Family: Cladorhizidae

Credit: NOAA/CINMS 2011

Asbestopluma sp.
sponge, branched (white)

Preliminary Identification: Tom Laidig
Identification Confirmation: Tom Laidig
Video Identifiability: Unconfirmed by video

Approximate Depth: 1,014m

1. Phylum: PORIFERA
1.2. Class: Hexactinellida
1.2.1. Order: Hexactinosida
1.2.1.1. Family: Aphrocallistidae

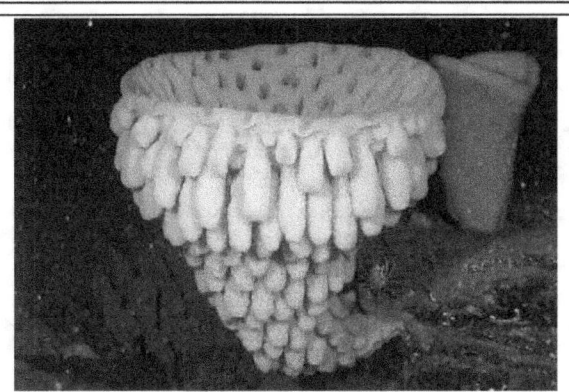

Credit: NOAA/CINMS 2011

Heterochone calyx
sponge, goiter (pink)

Preliminary Identification: J. Bright
Identification Confirmation: Tom Laidig
Video Identifiability: Confirmed

Approximate Depth: 786m

2. Phylum: CNIDARIA
  2.1. Class: Scyphozoa – jellyfish
    2.1.1. Subclass: Scyphomedusea
      2.1.1.1. Order: Semaeostomeae
        2.1.1.1.1. Family: Ulmaridae
          2.1.1.1.1.1 Subfamily: Poralunae

Credit: NOAA/CINMS 2011

Poralia rufescens (probably)
jellyfish

Prelilminary Identification: J. Bright
Identification Confirmation: Lonny
Lundsten
Video Identifiability: Unable from video

Approximate Depth: 786m

2. Phylum: CNIDARIA
  2.2. Class: Hydrozoa
    2.1.1. Order: Trachymedusae
      2.1.1.1. Family: Rhopalonematidae

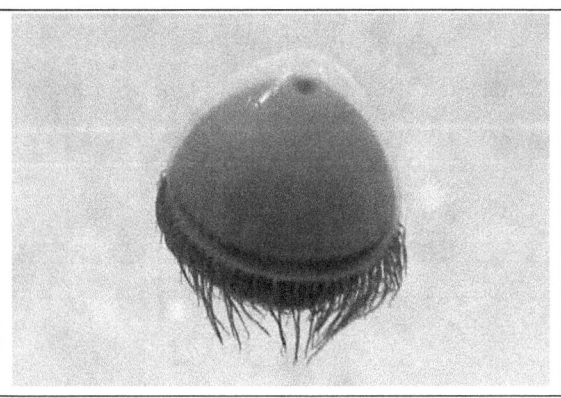

Credit: NOAA/CINMS 2011

Benthocodon sp.
jelly

Preliminary Classification: J. Bright
Identification Confirmation: Tom Laidig
Video Identifiability: Confirmed

Approximate Depth: 1,014m

2. Phylum: CNIDARIA
2.3. Class: Hydrozoa
2.3.1. Subclass: Siphonophorae – siphonophores
2.3.1.1. Order: Physonectae
2.3.1.1.1. Family: Apolemiidae

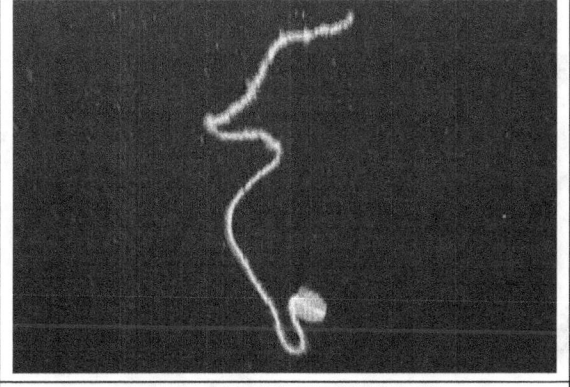

Credit: NOAA/CINMS 2011

Apolemia sp.
(possibly)

Preliminary Identification: J. Bright
Identification Confirmation:
Video Identifiability: Provisional

Approximate Depth: 1,014m

2. Phylum: CNIDARIA
2.3. Class: Hydrozoa
2.3.2. Subclass: Siphonophorae - siphonophores
2.3.2.1. Order: Physonectae
2.3.2.1.1. Family: Rhodaliidae

Credit: NOAA/CINMS 2011

Dromalia alexandri

siphonophore

Preliminary Classification: J. Bright
Identification Confirmation: Lonny Lundsten
Video Identifiability: Confirmed

Approximate Depth: 886m

2. Phylum: CNIDARIA
2.4. Class: Anthozoa
2.4.1. Subclass: Hexacorallia (Zoantharia)
2.4.1.1. Order: Actiniaria - anemones

ACTINIARIA species 1
burrowing sea anemone

Preliminary Identification: J. Bright
Identification Confirmation: D. Fautin, PhD.
Video Identifiability: Unable from video

Approximate Depth: 886m

Credit: NOAA/CINMS 2011

2. Phylum: CNIDARIA
2.4. Class: Anthozoa
2.4.1. Subclass: Hexacorallia (Zoantharia)
2.4.1.1. Order: Actiniaria – anemones
2.4.1.1.1. Suborder: Nyantheae

Credit: NOAA/CINMS 2011

ACTINIARIA species 2

anemone

Preliminary Identification: J. Bright
Identification Confirmation: D. Fautin, Phd.
Video Identifiability: Unable from video

Approximate Depth: 886m

Credit: NOAA/CINMS 2011

ACTINIARIA species 3

anemone

Preliminary Identification: J. Bright
Identification Confirmation: D. Fautin, PhD.
Video Identifiability: Unable from video

Approximate Depth: 786m

2. Phylum: CNIDARIA
2.4. Class: Anthozoa
2.4.2. Subclass: Hexacorallia (Zoantharia)
2.4.2.1. Order: Corallimorpharia
2.4.2.1.1. Family: Corallimorphidae

Corallimorphus pilatus
(Provisional by D. Fautin)

Preliminary Identification: J. Bright
Identification Confirmation: D. Fautin, PhD.
Video Identifiability: Unable from video

Approximate Depth: 745m

NOAA/CINMS 2011

2. Phylum: CNIDARIA
2.4. Class: Anthozoa
2.4.2. Subclass: Hexacorallia (Zoantharia)
2.4.3. Order: Actiniaria – anemones
2.4.3.1. Suborder: Nyantheae
####### 2.4.3.1.1. Family: Liponematidae

	*Liponema brevicornis* pom pom anemone Preliminary Identification: J. Bright Identification Confirmation: D. Fautin, PhD. Video Identifiability: Confirmed Approximate Depth: 745m
Credit: NOAA/CINMS 2011	

2. Phylum: CNIDARIA
2.4. Class: Anthozoa
2.4.3. Subclass: Octocorallia (Alcyonaria)
2.4.3.1. Order: Alcyonacea – soft corals
2.4.3.1.1. Suborder: Alcyoniina
2.4.3.1.1.1. Family: Alcyoniidae

	*Anthomastus* sp. mushroom coral Preliminary Identification: J. Bright Identification Confirmation: Tom Laidig Video Identifiability: Confirmed Approximate Depth: 786m
NOAA/CINMS 2011	
	*Anthomastus ritteri* mushroom coral Preliminary Identification: J. Bright Identification Confirmation: Tom Laidig Video Identifiability: Confirmed Approximate Depth: 1,014m
NOAA/CINMS 2011	

2. Phylum: CNIDARIA
2.4. Class: Anthozoa
2.4.3. Subclass: Octocorallia
2.4.3.1. Order: Alcyonacea

17

	PENNATULACEA sea pen Preliminary Identification: J. Bright Identification Confirmation: Video Identifiability: Provisional Approximate Depth: 745m
Credit: NOAA/CINMS 2011	

2. Phylum: CNIDARIA
   2.4. Class: Anthozoa
      2.4.3.1. Subclass: Octocorallia
         2.5.1.1. Order: Pennatulacea – sea pens
            2.5.1.1.1. Suborder: Subsessiliflorae

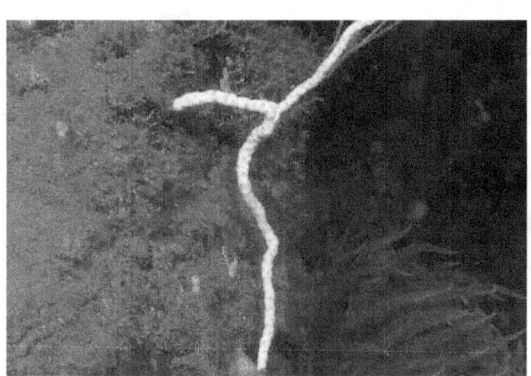 Credit: NOAA/CINMS 2011	Suborder: Scleraxonia Family: Paragorgiidae *Paragorgia* sp. paragorgia (white) Preliminary Identification: J. Bright Identification Confirmation: Tom Laidig Video Identifiability: Unconfirmed by video Approximate Depth: 1,014m
 Credit: NOAA/CINMS 2011	Suborder: Holaxonia Family: Plexauridae *Swiftia* type (no specimens collected) Preliminary Identification: J. Bright Identification Confirmation: Tom Laidig Video Identifiability: Unconfirmed by video
 Credit: NOAA/CINMS 2011	Suborder: Stolonifera Family: Clavulariidae *Clavularia* sp. Preliminary Identification: J. Bright Identification Confirmation: Tom Laidig Video Identifiability: Unconfirmed by video Approximate Depth: 1,014m

2. Phylum: CNIDARIA
2.4. Class: Anthozoa
2.4.3. Subclass: Octocorallia
2.5.1.1. Order: Pennatulacea – sea pens
2.5.1.1.1. Suborder: Subsessiliflorae

Credit: NOAA/CINMS 2011

Family: Umbellulidae
Umbellula lindahli
droopy sea pen

Preliminary Identification: J. Bright
Identification Confirmation:
Video Identifiability: Provisional

Approximate Depth: 745m

Credit: NOAA/CINMS 2011

Family: Halipteridae
Halipteris californica
sea pen

Preliminary Identification: J. Bright
Identification Confirmation:
Video Identifiability: Provisional

Approximate Depth: 886m

Credit: NOAA/CINMS 2011

Family: Pennatulidae
Pennatula phosphorea
phosphorescent sea pen

Preliminary Identification: J. Bright
Identification Confirmation:
Video Identifiability: Provisional

Approximate Depth: 886m

3. Phylum: MOLLUSCA – slugs, chitons, clams, squids, octopuses

    3.1. Class: Gastropoda

        3.1.1. Subclass: Opisthobranchia - nudibranchs

            3.1.1.1. Order: Nudibranchia

                3.1.1.1.1. Family: Tritoniidae

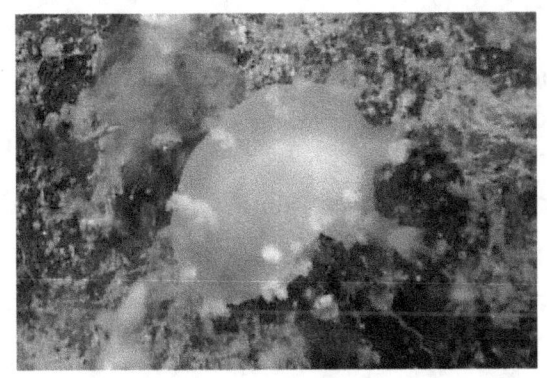

Tritonia sp.
nudibranch

Preliminary Classification: J. Bright
Identification Confirmation: Lonny Lundsten
Video Identifiability: Confirmed

Approximate Depth: 1,014m

Credit: NOAA/CINMS 2011

3. Phylum: MOLLUSCA
3.1. Class: Gastropoda
3.1.2. Order: Vetigastropoda
3.1.2.1. Superfamily: Seguenzioidea
3.1.2.1.1. Family: Calliotropidae

Bathybembix sp.

Preliminary Classification: J. Bright
Identification Confirmation: Lonny Lundsten
Video Identifiability: Unconfirmed from video

Approximate Depth: 886m

Credit: NOAA/CINMS 2011

3. Phylum: MOLLUSCA
   3.1. Class: Gastropoda
      3.2.1. Order: Caenogastropoda
         3.2.1.1. Suborder: Neogastropoda
            3.2.1.1.1. Family: Buccinidae – sea snails

Credit: NOAA/CINMS 2011

Neptunea sp.

Preliminary Classification: J. Bright
Identification Confirmation: Lonny Lundsten
Video Identifiability: Confirmed

Approximate Depth: 886m

3. Phylum: MOLLUSCA
 3.2. Class: Bivalvia - bivalves
  3.2.1. Subclass: Pteriomorphia
   3.2.1.1. Order: Ostreoida
    3.2.1.1.1. Family: Pectinidae - scallops

Credit: NOAA/CINMS 2011

Pectinidae sp.
scallop

Preliminary Identification: J. Bright
Identification Confirmation:
Video Identifiability: Provisional

Approximate Depth: 745m

3. Phylum: MOLLUSCA
3.3. Class: Cephalopoda
3.3.1. Subclass: Coleoidea
3.3.1.1. Superorder: Octobrachia
3.3.1.1.1. Order: Octopoda - octopus
3.3.1.1.1.1. Suborder: Incirrina
####### 3.3.1.1.1.1.1. Family: Octopodidae
######## 3.3.1.1.1.1.1.1. Subfamily: Octopodinae

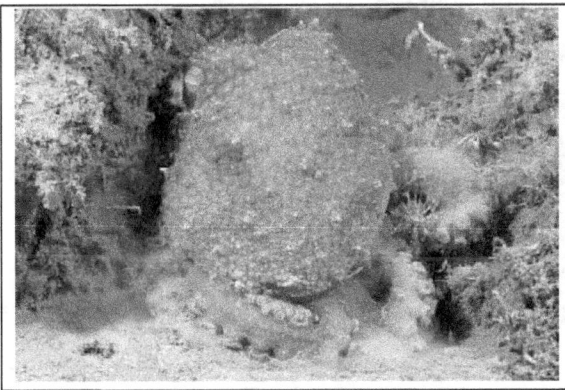

Credit: NOAA/CINMS 2011

Enteroctopus dofleini
giant Pacific octopus

Preliminary Identification: J. Bright
Identification Confirmation: Tom Laidig
Video Identifiability: Confirmed

Approximate Depth: 786m

4. Phylum: ANNELIDA – segmented worms

4.1. Class: Polychaeta – polychaete worms
4.1.1. Subclass: Palpata
4.1.1.1. Order: Aciculata
4.1.1.1.1. Suborder: Phyllodocida
####### 4.1.1.1.1.1. Family: Polynoidae

Credit: NOAA/CINMS 2011

POLYNOIDAE
scale worm, red

Preliminary Identification: J. Bright
Identification Confirmation: Tom Laidig
Video Identifiability: Unconfirmed from video

Approximate Depth: 886m

5. Phylum: ARTHROPODA – sea spiders, barnacles, shrimps, crabs

5.1. Subphylum: Chelicerata
5.1.1. Class: Pycnogonida – sea spiders

Credit: NOAA/CINMS 2011

PYCNOGONIDA
sea spider

Preliminary Identification: J. Bright
Identification Confirmation:
Video Identifiability: Provisional

Approximate Depth: 886m

5. Phylum: ARTHROPODA
5.2. Subphylum: Crustacea – crustaceans
5.2.1. Class: Malacostraca
5.2.1.1. Subclass: Eumalacostraca
5.2.1.1.1. Superorder: Eucarida
####### 5.2.1.1.1.1. Order: Decapoda – shrimp, lobsters, crabs
######## 5.2.1.1.1.1.1. Suborder: Pleocyemata
######### 5.2.1.1.1.1.1.1. Infraorder: Caridea

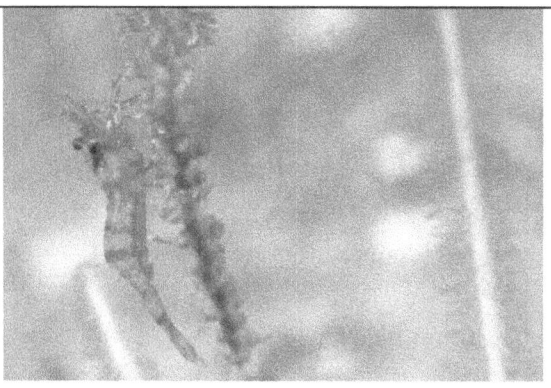 Credit: NOAA/CINMS 2011	CARIDEA shrimp Preliminary Identification: J. Bright Identification Confirmation: Video Identifiability: Provisional Approximate Depth: 1,014m
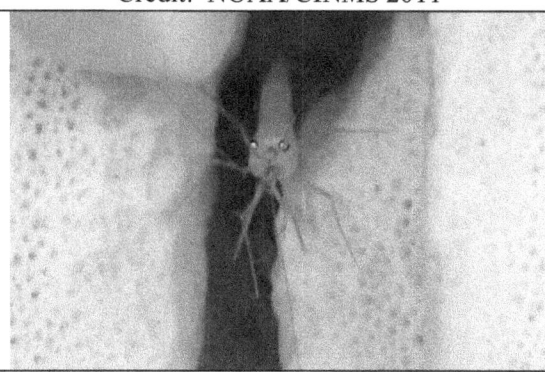Credit: NOAA/CINMS 2011	Family: Pandalidae *Pandalopsis ampla* shrimp, deep water Preliminary Identification: J. Bright Identification Confirmation: Video Identifiability: Provisional Approximate Depth: 786m

5. Phylum: ARTHROPODA

    5.2. Subphylum: Crustacea –crustaceans

        5.2.2. Class: Malacostraca

            5.2.2.2. Subclass: Eumalacostraca

                5.3.1.1.1. Superorder: Peracarida

                    5.3.1.1.1.1. Order: Mysida - mysids

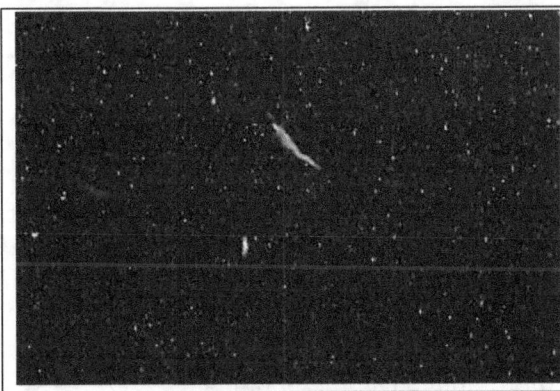

Credit: NOAA/CINMS 2011

MYSIDA

shrimp, opossum

Preliminary Identification: J. Bright

Identification Confirmation:

Video Identifiability: Unconfirmed by video

Approximate Depth: 786m

5. Phylum: ARTHROPODA

    5.2. Subphylum: Crustacea – crustaceans
        5.2.3. Class: Malacostraca
            5.2.3.3. Subclass: Eumalacostraca
                5.2.3.1.1. Superorder: Eucarida
                    5.2.3.1.1.1. Order: Decapoda – shrimp, lobsters, crabs
                        5.2.3.1.1.1. Suborder: Pleocyemata
                            5.2.3.1.1.1.1. Infraorder: Anomura
                              5.2.3.1.1.1.1.1. Family: Lithodidae – king crabs

Credit: NOAA/CINMS 2011

Lithodes cousei
scarlet king crab

Preliminary Identification: J. Bright
Identification Confirmation: Greg Jensen, PhD.
Video Identifiability: Confirmed

Approximate Depth: 886m

Credit: NOAA/CINMS 2011

Lithodes cousei
scarlet king crab

Preliminary Identification: J. Bright
Identification Confirmation: Lonny Lundsten
Video Identifiability: Confirmed

Approximate Depth: 786m

5. Phylum: ARTHROPODA

    5.2. Subphylum: Crustacea - crustaceans

        5.2.3. Class: Malacostraca

            5.2.3.4. Subclass: Eumalacostraca

                5.2.3.4.2. Superorder: Eucarida

                    5.2.3.4.2.2. Order: Decapoda – shrimps, lobsters, crabs

                        5.2.3.4.2.2.1. Suborder: Pleocyemata

                            5.2.3.4.2.2.1.1. Infraorder: Anomura

                                5.2.3.4.2.2.1.1.1. Family: Galatheidae

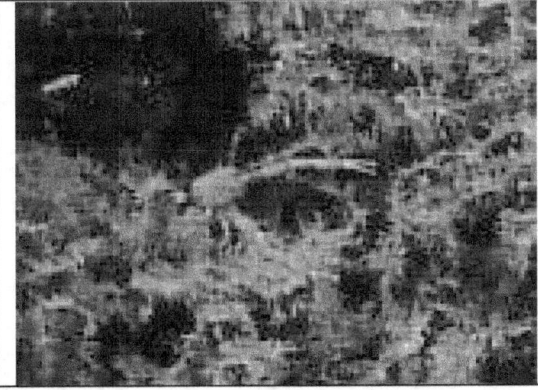

Credit: NOAA/CINMS 2011

Munida sp.
squat lobster

Preliminary Identification: J. Bright
Identification Confirmation: Linda Kuhnz
Video Identifiability: Confirmed

Approximate Depth: 1,014m

5. Phylum: ARTHROPODA
5.2 Subphylum: Crustacea - crustaceans
5.2.3. Class: Malacostraca
5.2.3.4. Subclass: Eumalacostraca
5.2.3.4.2. Superorder: Eucarida
####### 5.2.3.4.2.2. Order: Decapoda – shrimps, lobsters, crabs
######## 5.2.3.4.2.2.2. Suborder: Pleocyemata
######### 5.2.3.4.2.2.2.1. Infraorder: Brachyura
########## 5.2.3.4.2.2.2.1.1. Superfamily: Majoidea
########### 5.2.3.4.2.2.2.1.1.1. Family: Majidae

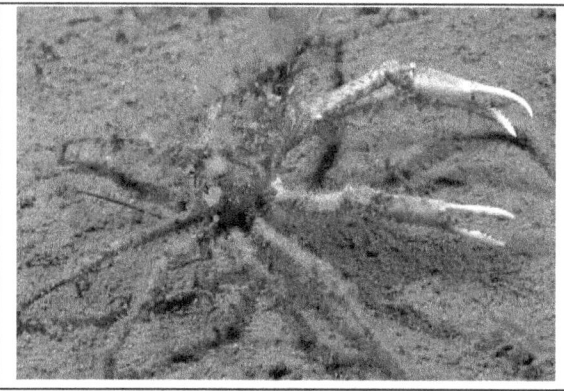

Credit: NOAA/CINMS 2011

Chorilia longipes
long horned decorator crab

Preliminary Identification: J. Bright
Identification Confirmation: Lonny Lundsten
Video Identifiability: Confirmed

Approximate Depth: 886m

5. Phylum: ARTHROPODA

    5.2. Subphylum: Crustacea - crustaceans

        5.2.3. Class: Malacostraca

            5.2.3.4. Subclass: Eumalacostraca

                5.2.3.4.2. Superorder: Eucarida

                    5.2.3.4.2.2. Order: Decapoda – shrimps, lobsters, crabs

                        5.2.3.4.2.2.2. Suborder: Pleocyemata

                            5.2.3.4.2.2.2.1. Infraorder: Brachyura

                                5.2.3.4.2.2.2.1.1. Superfamily: Majoidea

                                    5.2.3.4.2.2.2.1.1.2. Family: Oregoniidae

Chionoecetes tanneri
grooved tanner crab

Preliminary Identification: Lonny Lundsten
Identification Confirmation: Lonny Lundsten
Video Identifiability: Confirmed

Approximate Depth: 886m

Credit: NOAA/CINMS 2011

5. Phylum: ARTHROPODA

  5.2. Subphylum: Crustacea – crustaceans
    5.2.3. Class: Malacostraca
      5.2.3.4. Subclass: Eumalacostraca
        5.2.3.4.3. Superorder: Peracarida
          5.2.3.4.3.1. Order: Isopoda - isopods

	ISOPODA isopod (possibly Suborder: Valvifera) Preliminary Identification: J. Bright Identification Confirmation: M. Wicksten, PhD. Video Identifiability: Unable from video Approximate Depth: 886m
Credit: NOAA/CINMS 2011	

5. Phylum: ARTHROPODA

  5.2. Subphylum: Crustacea – crustaceans

      5.2.3. Class: Malacostraca

          5.2.3.4. Subclass: Eumalacostraca

             5.2.3.4.3. Superorder: Peracarida

                 5.2.3.4.3.1. Order: Amphipoda

                    5.2.3.4.3.1.1. Suborder: Gammaridea

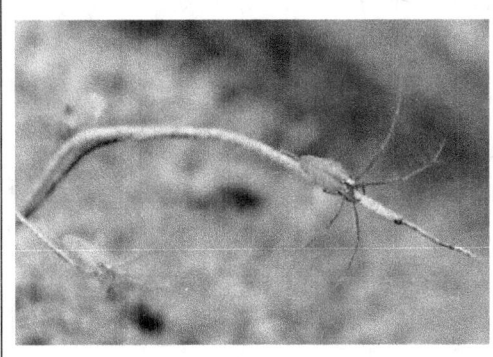

Credit: NOAA/CINMS 2011

GAMMARID
amphipod

Preliminary Identification: J. Bright
Identification Confirmation: M. Wicksten, PhD.
Video Identifiability: Unconfirmed from Video

Approximate Depth: 886m

5. Phylum: ARTHROPODA
5.2. Subphylum: Crustacea – crustaceans
5.2.3. Class: Malacostraca
5.2.3.4. Subclass: Eumalacostraca
####### 5.2.3.4.4. Superorder: Caprellidea - caprellid
######## 5.2.3.4.4.1. Infraorder: Caprellida
######### 5.2.3.4.4.1.1. Family: Caprellidae

Credit: NOAA/CINMS 2011

Caprellidae sp.
skeleton shrimp

Preliminary Identification: J. Bright
Identification Confirmation: Tom Laidig
Video Identifiability: Confirmed

Approximate Depth: 886m

6. Phylum: ECHINODERMATA

6.1. Class: Crinoidea – crinoids, feather stars
6.1.1. Subclass: Articulata
6.1.1.1. Order: Comatulida
6.1.1.1.1. Family: Antedonidae

NOAA/CINMS 2011

Florometra serratissima
Crinoid (feather star)

Preliminary Identification: J. Bright
Identification Comfirmation:
Video Identifiability: Provisional

Approximate Depth: 886m

6. Phylum: ECHINODERMATA
6.2. Subphylum: Asterozoa
6.2.1. Class: Asteroidea – sea stars
6.2.1.1. Superorder: Valvatacea
6.2.1.1.1. Order: Valvatida

Credit: NOAA/CINMS 2011

Family: Goniasteridae
Ceramaster leptoceramus
California cookie star

Preliminary Identification: J. Bright
Identification Confirmation:
Video Identifiability: Provisional

Approximate Depth: 745m

Credit: NOAA/CINMS 2011

Family: Goniasteridae
Gephyreaster swifti
sea star

Preliminary Identification: J. Bright
Identification Confirmation:
Video Identifiability: Provisional

Approximate Depth: 745m

Credit: NOAA/CINMS 2011

Family: Poraniidae
Poraniopsis sp.
thorny star

Preliminary Identification: J. Bright
Identification Confirmation:
Video Identifiability: Provisional

Approximate Depth: 745m

6. Phylum: ECHINODERMATA
6.2. Subphylum: Asterozoa
6.2.1. Class: Asteroidea – sea stars
6.2.1.1. Superorder: Valvatacea
6.2.2.1.1. Order: Velatida
####### 6.2.2.1.1.1. Family: Solasteridae

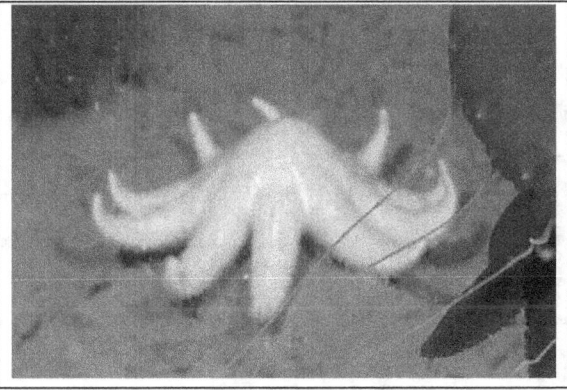

Credit: NOAA/CINMS 2011

Solaster sp.

sea star

Preliminary Identification: J. Bright

Identification Confirmation: Phil Lambert

Video Identifiability: Provisional

Approximate Depth: 745m

6. Phylum: ECHINODERMATA
6.2. Subphylum: Asterozoa
6.2.1. Class: Asteroidea – sea stars
6.3.1.1. Superorder: Spinulosacea
6.3.1.1.1. Order: Spinulosida
####### 6.3.1.1.1.1. Family: Echinasteridae

Credit: NOAA/CINMS 2011

Henricia sanguinolenta
sea star

Preliminary Identification: J. Bright
Identification Confirmation:
Video Identifiability: Provisional

Approximate Depth: 745m

6. Phylum: ECHINODERMATA

6.2. Subphylum: Asterozoa
6.2.1. Class: Asteroidea – sea stars
6.4.1. Order: Forcipulatida
6.4.1.1. Family: Zoroasteridae

Credit: NOAA/CINMS 2011

Zoroaster sp.
sea star, pink

Preliminary Identification: J. Bright
Identification Confirmation:
Video Identifiability: Provisional

Approximate Depth: 1,014m

6. Phylum: ECHINODERMATA

6.2. Subphylum: Asterozoa
6.2.1. Class: Asteroidea – sea stars
6.5.1. Superorder: Forcipulatacea
6.5.1.1. Order: Brisingida
6.5.1.1.1. Family: Brisingidae

Credit: NOAA/CINMS 2011

BRISINGIDAE
sea star, brisingid

Preliminary Classification: J. Bright
Identification Confirmation:
Video Identifiability: Provisional

Approximate Depth: 745m

6. Phylum: ECHINODERMATA
6.2. Subphylum: Asterozoa
6.3.1. Class: Ophiuroidea – brittle stars, basket stars
6.3.1.1. Order: Ophiurida
6.3.1.1.1. Suborder: Ophiurina

 Credit: NOAA/CINMS 2011	Family: Ophiacanthidae *Ophiacantha* sp. brittle star Preliminary Identification: J. Bright Identification Confirmation: Video Identifiability: Provisional Approximate Depth: 745m
 Credit: NOAA/CINMS 2011	Family: Ophiolepididae *Ophiomusium jolliensis* red brittle star Preliminary Identification: J. Bright Identification Confirmation: Video Identifiability: Provisional Approximate Depth: 745m

6. Phylum: ECHINODERMATA
6.4. Subphylum: Echinozoa
6.4.1. Class: Echinoidea
6.4.1.1. Subclass: Euechinoidea
6.4.1.1.1. Infraclass: Carinacea
####### 6.4.1.1.1. 1. Superorder: Echinacea
####### 6.4.1.1.1. 1.1. Order: Camarodonta
####### 6.4.1.1.1. 1.1.1. Infraorder: Echinidea
####### 6.4.1.1.1. 1.1.1.1. Superfamily: Odontophora
####### 6.4.1.1.1. 1.1.1.1.1. Family: Strongylocentrotidae

Strongylocentrotus fragilis
pink sea urchin

Preliminary Identification: J. Bright
Identification Confirmation:
Video Identifiability: Provisional

Approximate Depth: 786m

NOAA/CINMS 2011

43

6. Phylum: ECHINODERMATA

6.4. Subphylum: Echinozoa
6.4.1. Class: Holothuroidea – sea cucumbers
6.4.1.1. Subclass: Dendrochirotacea
6.4.1.1.1. Order: Dendrochirotida
####### 6.4.1.1.1.1. Family: Psolidae

NOAA/CINMS 2011

Psolus squamatus
sea cucumber

Preliminary Identification: J. Bright
Identification Confirmation: Lonny Lundsten
Video Identifiability: Confirmed

Approximate Depth: 803m

6. Phylum: ECHINODERMATA
6.4. Subphylum: Echinozoa
6.4.2. Class: Holothuroidea – sea cucumbers
6.4.2.1. Order: Elasipodida
6.4.2.1.1. Family: Laetmogonidae

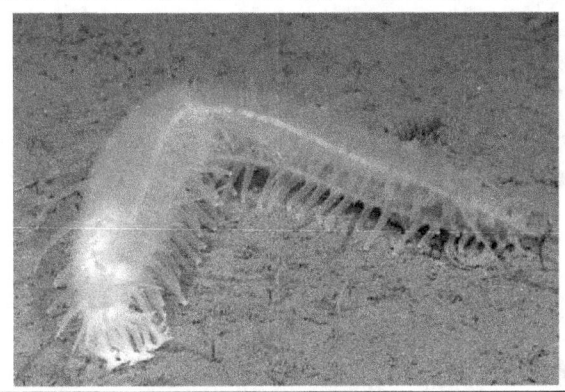

NOAA/CINMS 2011

Pannychia moseleyi
Sea cucumber

Preliminary Identification: J. Bright
Identification Confirmation: Phil Lambert
Video Identifiability: Confirmed

Approximate Depth: 803m

7. Phylum: CHORDATA

7.1 Subphylum: Tunicata
7.1.1. Class: Ascidiacea
7.1.1.1. Order: Phlebobranchia

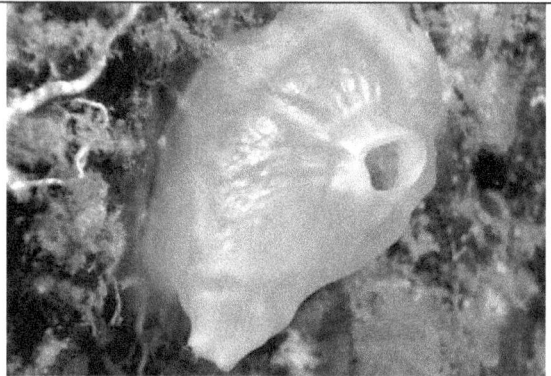

Credit: NOAA/CINMS 2011

Family: Pyuridae
Halocynthia aurantium
sea squirt or sea peach

Preliminary Identification: J. Bright
Identification Confirmation:
Video Identifiability: Provisional

Approximate Depth: 745m

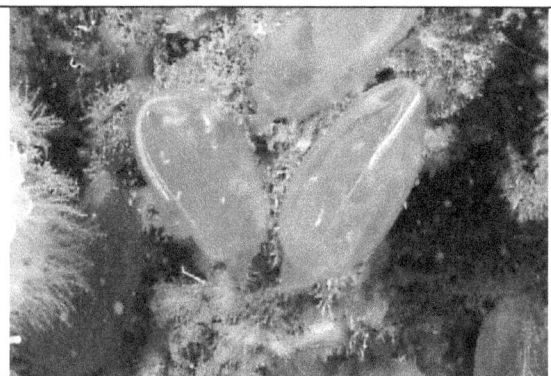

Credit: NOAA/CINMS 2011

Family: Corellidae
Corella inflata
brooding transparent tunicate

Preliminary Identification: J. Bright
Identification Confirmation:
Video Identifiability: Provisional

Approximate Depth: 786m

7. Phylum: CHORDATA
    7.1 Subphylum: Tunicata
        7.1.1. Class: Ascidiacea
            7.1.1.1. Order: Phlebobranchia
                7.1.1.1.2. Family: Octacnemidae

	*Megalodicopia hians* predatory tunicate Preliminary Identification: Identification Confirmation: Tom Laidig Video Identifiability: Confirmed Approximate Depth: 1,014m
Credit: NOAA/CINMS 2011	

7. Phylum: CHORDATA
7.2. Subphylum: Vertebrata
7.2.1. Class: Chrondrichthyes – cartilaginous fishes
7.2.1.1. Subclass: Elasmobranchii
7.2.1.1.1. Order: Carcharhiniformes
####### 7.2.1.1.1.1. Family: Scyliorhinidae

 Credit: NOAA/CINMS 2011	*Apristurus brunneus* brown cat shark Preliminary Identification: J. Bright Identification Confirmation: Tom Laidig Video Identifiabillity: Confirmed Approximate Depth: 803m
 Credit: NOAA/CINMS 2011	*Apristurus brunneus* (juvenile) brown cat shark Preliminary Identification: J. Bright Identification Confirmation: Tom Laidig Video Identifiability: Confirmed Approximate Depth: 786m

7. Phylum: CHORDATA

7.2. Class: Chondrichthyes– cartilaginous fishes
7.2.2. Order: Rajiformes
7.2.2.1. Family: Rajidae

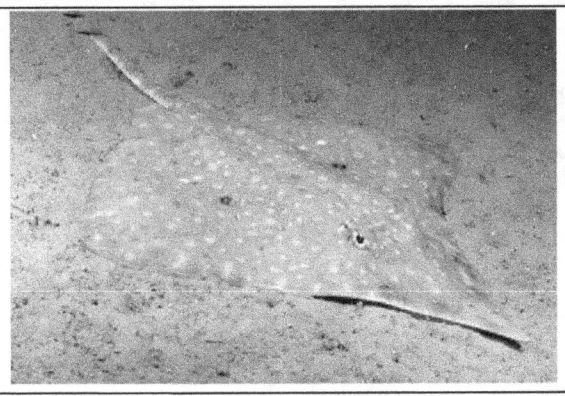

Credit: NOAA/CINMS 2011

Raja rhina
longnose skate

Preliminary Classification: J. Bright
Identification Confirmation: Tom Laidig
Video Identifiability: Confirmed

Approximate Depth: 786m

7. Phylum: CHORDATA
    7.4. Subphylum: Vertebrata
        7.4.1. Superclass: Agnatha
            7.4.1.1. Class: Myxini
                7.4.1.1.1. Order: Myxiniformes
                    7.4.1.1.1.1. Family: Myxinidae
                        7.4.1.1.1.1.1. Subfamily: Eptatretinae

Credit: NOAA/CINMS 2011

Eptatretus stoutii
Pacific hagfish

Preliminary Identification: J. Bright
Identification Confirmation: Tom Laidig
Video Identifiatility: Confirmed

Approximate Depth: 886m

7. Phylum: CHORDATA
7.4. Subphylum: Vertebrata
7.4.2. Superclass: Osteichthyes – bony fishes
7.4.2.1. Class: Actinopterygii – ray-finned fishes
7.4.2.1.1. Order: Gadiformes
7.4.2.1.1.1. Family: Moridae – codlings

Credit: NOAA/CINMS 2011

Antimora microlepis
codling, finescale (or Pacific flatnose)

Preliminary Classification: J. Bright
Identification Confirmation:
Video Identifiability: Provisional

Approximate Depth: 1,014m

7. Phylum: CHORDATA
7.4. Subphylum: Vertebrata
7.4.2. Superclass: Osteichthyes
7.4.2.2. Class: Actinopterygii
7.4.2.2.2. Subclass: Neopterygii
7.4.2.2.2.2. Order: Scorpaeniformes
####### 7.4.2.2.2.2.2. Family: Scorpaenidae – scorpionfishes and rockfishes

Credit: NOAA/CINMS 2011

Sebastolobus alascanus
shortspine thornyhead

Preliminary Identification: J. Bright
Identification Confirmation: Tom Laidig
Video Identifiability: Confirmed

Approximate Depth: 786m

7. Phylum: CHORDATA
7.4. Subphylum: Vertebrata
7.4.2. Superclass: Osteichthyes
7.4.2.2. Class: Actinopterygii
7.4.2.2.2. Subclass: Neopterygii
7.4.2.2.2.2. Order: Scorpaeniformes
####### 7.4.2.2.2.2.2. Family: Scorpaenidae – scorpionfishes and rockfishes

Credit: NOAA/CINMS 2011

Sebastolobus altivelis
longspine thornyhead

Preliminary Identification:
Identification Confirmation: Tom Laidig
Video Identifiability: Confirmed

Approximate Depth: 745m

Credit: NOAA/CINMS 2011

Sebastolobus altivelis
longspine thornyhead (juvenile)

Preliminary Identification:
Identification Confirmation: Tom Laidig
Video Identifiability: Confirmed

Approximate Depth: 886m

7. Phylum: CHORDATA
7.4. Subphylum: Vertebrata
7.4.2. Superclass: Osteichthyes
7.4.2.2. Class: Actinopterygii
7.4.2.2.2. Subclass: Neopterygii
7.4.2.2.2.2. Order: Scorpaeniformes
####### 7.4.2.2.2.2.3 Family: Agonidae

Xeneretmus leiops
smootheye poacher

Preliminary Identification: J. Bright
Identification Confirmation: Tom Laidig
Video Identifiability: Confirmed

Approximate Depth: 786m

Credit: NOAA/CINMS 2011

7. Phylum: CHORDATA
7.4. Subphylum: Verbrata
7.4.2. Superclass: Osteichthyes
7.4.2.2. Class: Actinopterygii
7.4.2.2.3. Order: Pleuronectiformes
####### 7.4.2.2.3.1. Family: Paralichyidae – left eye flounder

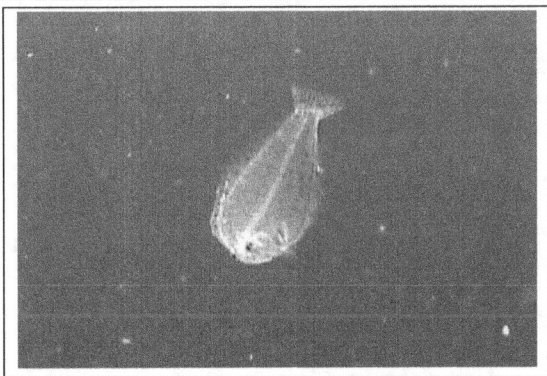

Credit: NOAA/CINMS 2011

Citharichthys sordidus

Preliminary Identification: J. Bright
Identification Confirmation: Tom Laidig
Video Identifiability: Unable from video

Approximate Depth: 786m

7. Phylum: CHORDATA

7.4. Subphylum: Verbrata
7.4.2. Superclass: Osteichthyes
7.4.2.2. Class: Actinopterygii
7.4.2.2.3. Order: Pleuronectiformes
####### 7.4.2.2.3.2. Suborder: Pleuronectoidei
######## 7.4.2.2.3.2.1. Family: Pleuronectidae – right eye flounders

 Credit: NOAA/CINMS 2011	*Microstomus pacificus* dover sole Preliminary Identification: J. Bright Identification Confirmation: Tom Laidig Video Identifiability: Confirmed Approximate Depth: 786m
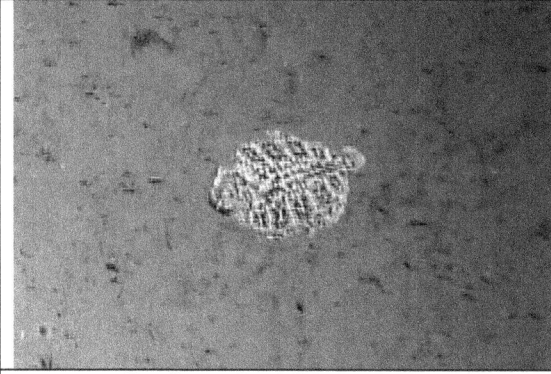Credit: NOAA/CINMS 2011	*Embassichthys bathybius* deepsea sole Preliminary Identification: J. Bright Identification Confirmation: Tom Laidig Video Identifiability: Confirmed Approximate Depth: 1,014m

7. Phylum: CHORDATA

7.4. Subphylum: Vertebrata
7.4.2. Superclass: Osteichthyes – bony fishes
7.4.2.2. Class: Actinopterygii - ray-finned fishes
7.4.2.2.4. Order: Perciformes
####### 7.4.2.2.4.1. Family: Zoarcidae - eelpouts

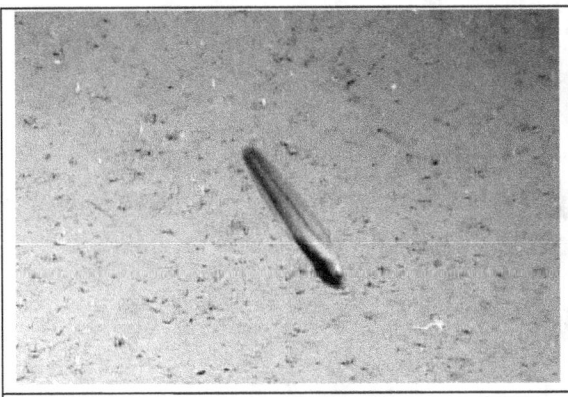

NOAA/CINMS 2011

ZOARCIDAE spp.

eelpout

Preliminary Classification:

Identification Confirmation: Tom Laidig

Video Identifiability: Confirmed

Approximate Depth: 745m

7. Phylum: CHORDATA

7.4. Subphylum: Vertebrata
7.4.2. Superclass: Osteichthyes – bony fishes
7.4.2.2. Class: Actinopterygii - ray-finned fishes
7.4.2.2.4. Order: Perciformes
7.4.2.2.4.1. Family: Zoarcidae - eelpouts

Credit: NOAA/CINMS 2011

Lycenchelys crotalinus
eelpout, snakehead

Preliminary Identification: J. Bright
Identification Confirmation: Tom Laidig
Video Identifiability: Confirmed

Approximate Depth: 886m

Credit: NOAA/CINMS 2011

Lycodapus mandibularis
eelpout, pallid

Preliminary Identification: J. Bright
Identification Confirmation: Tom Laidig
Video Identifiability: Unconfirmed from video

Approximate Depth: 886m

REFERENCES

Behrens, D.W. 1991. Pacific Coast Nudibranchs, Second Edition, Sea Challengers, Monterey, CA. 107 pages.

Boury-Esnault, N., and Klaus Rutzler (editors). 1997. Thesaurus of sponge morphology. Smithsonian Contributions to Zoology, number 596.

Burton, Erica J., and L. Lundsten. 2008. Davidson Seamount Taxonomic Guide. Marine Sanctuaries Conservation Series ONMS 08-08. 145 pages.

Butler, J.L., M. Love, T. Laidig. 2012. A Guide to the Rockfishes, thornyheads and Scorpionfishes of the Northeast Pacific. University of California Press, Berkeley, Los Angeles, CA. 185 pages.

Gotshall, D.W. 1994. Guide to Marine Invertebrates: Alaska to Baja California, Sea Challengers, Monterey, CA. 105 pages.

Harbo, R.M. 1997. Shells and Shellfish of the Pacific Northwest, Harbour Publishing, Madeira Park, BC, Canada. 270 pages.

Integrated Taxonomic Information System (ITIS). World Wide Web electronic publication. [www.itis.gov]. Accessed [09-01-2012 through 02-01-2013].

Khoyatan Marine Laboratory. World Wide Web electronic publication. [www.mareco.org/kml/sponges]. Accessed [09-01-2012 through 02-01-2013].

Kramer, D. E.et al. 1995. Guide to Northeast Pacific Flatfishes. Marine Advisory Bulletin. No. 47. 104 pages.

Lambert, P. 1997. Sea Cucumbers of British Columbia, Southeast Alaska and Puget Sound. Royal British Columbia Museum, Victoria, Canada. 166 pages.

Lambert, P. 2000. Sea Stars of British Columbia, Southeast Alaska and Puget Sound. Royal British Columbia Museum. Victoria, Canada. 186 pages.

Lambert, P. 2007. Brittle Stars, Sea Urchins and Feather Stars of British Columbia, Southeast Alaska and Puget Sound. Royal British Columbia Museum. Victoria, Canada. 150 pages.

Lipski, D.L., S.Katz, J.Bright. 2013. A Characterization of Deep-Sea Coral and Sponge Communities on the Continental Shelf of Channel Islands National Marine Sanctuary Using a Remotely Operated Vehicle.

Love, M. 2011. Certainly More Than You Want to Know About the Fishes of the Pacific Coast. Really Big Press, Santa Barbara, CA. 649 pages.

Love, M.S. et al. 2002. The Rockfishes of the Northeast Pacific. University of California Press, Berkeley and Los Angeles, CA. 404 pages.

Stone, R.P. et al. 2011. A Guide to the Deep-Water Sponges of the Aleutian Island Archipelago. NOAA Professional Paper NMFS 12. 187 pages.

World Register of Marine Species (WoRMS). World Wide Web electronic publication. [www.marinespecies.org]. Accessed [09-01-2012 through 02-01-2013].

Wrobel, D. and Claudia Mills. 1998. Pacific Coast Pelagic Invertebrates: A guide to the Common Gelatinous Animals. Sea Challengers, Monterey, CA. 108 pages.

PERSONAL COMMUNICATIONS

Antrim, Liam. Olympic Coast National Marine Sanctuary, Port Angeles, WA.
Fautin, Daphne, PhD. University of Kansas, Lawrence, KS.
Jensen, Gregory, PhD. University of Washington, Seattle, WA.
Kuhnz, Linda. Monterey Bay Aquarium Research Institute, Moss Landing, CA.
Laidig, Tom. Southwest Fisheries Science Center, NOAA, Santa Cruz, CA, .
Lambert, Phil. Royal British Columbia Museum, Victoria, BC, Canada (retired).
Lipski, Danielle. Channel Islands National Marine Sanctuary, Santa Barbara, CA.
Lundsten, Lonny. Monterey Bay Aquarium Research Institute, Moss Landing, CA.
Wicksten, Mary, PhD. Texas A & M University, College Station, TX.

ACKNOWLEDGEMENTS

The authors thank NOAA's Deep Sea Coral Research and Technology Program for providing funding to CINMS for the analysis of the *Okeanos Explorer* video. We also send a special thanks to experts who generously helped with species identification. Especially, a special thanks to Tom Laidig, NOAA's Southwest Fisheries Science Center, for his valuable contribution in helping confirm and identify organisms; Lonny Lundsten and Linda Kunhz from MBARI for their contributions in taxonomic identification; and Dr. Daphne Fautin taking time to review all the anemone images.

Also, we thank Ed Bowlby, Carol Bernthal, George Galasso, Kevin Grant, and Norma Klein with Olympic Coast National Marine Sanctuary (OCNMS) who all supported Jennifer working on this project at the OCNMS offices. Jennifer Bright thanks Danielle Lipski with Channel Islands National Marine Sanctuary for giving her the opportunity to work on this guide.

Finally, thanks is due to the anonymous peer reviewers of this document who provided comments and edits to the final draft.

www.ingramcontent.com/pod-product-compliance
Lightning Source LLC
Chambersburg PA
CBHW080438290526
45791CB00008BA/2549